EMMANUEL JOSEPH

The Legacy of Global Power Struggles

Copyright © 2025 by Emmanuel Joseph

All rights reserved. No part of this publication may be reproduced, stored or transmitted in any form or by any means, electronic, mechanical, photocopying, recording, scanning, or otherwise without written permission from the publisher. It is illegal to copy this book, post it to a website, or distribute it by any other means without permission.

First edition

This book was professionally typeset on Reedsy.
Find out more at reedsy.com

Contents

1. Chapter 1: The Dawn of Empires — 1
2. Chapter 2: The Rise of European Powers — 3
3. Chapter 3: The Ottoman Empire's Influence — 5
4. Chapter 4: The Colonial Legacy in Africa — 7
5. Chapter 5: The Cold War's Global Impact — 10
6. Chapter 6: The Rise of China — 13
7. Chapter 7: The Influence of the British Empire — 15
8. Chapter 8: The Influence of the Soviet Union — 18
9. Chapter 9: The American Century — 21
10. Chapter 10: The Impact of Decolonization — 24
11. Chapter 11: The Middle East and the Legacy of Empire — 27
12. Chapter 12: The Future of Global Power Struggles — 30

1

Chapter 1: The Dawn of Empires

The inception of empires marked a significant turning point in human history, altering the political, cultural, and economic landscapes of the world. Ancient civilizations such as Mesopotamia, Egypt, and the Indus Valley laid the groundwork for what would become vast, sprawling empires that shaped the course of history. These early empires were built on the foundations of centralized power, technological advancements, and military prowess. The legacy of these ancient powerhouses continues to influence contemporary international relations, as the strategies and tactics they employed are still studied and emulated by modern states.

The Sumerians of Mesopotamia are often credited with creating one of the first known civilizations. Their development of writing, complex social structures, and trade networks set the stage for future empires. The Egyptians, with their remarkable achievements in architecture, art, and governance, established a model for centralized authority that would be replicated by subsequent empires. Meanwhile, the Indus Valley Civilization, known for its advanced urban planning and sophisticated trade systems, demonstrated the potential for economic power to shape regional dynamics. These early empires laid the groundwork for the rise of larger, more influential powers.

As empires expanded, they encountered new cultures and societies, leading to the exchange of ideas, technologies, and practices. The Persian Empire, for example, is renowned for its administrative innovations and multicultural approach to governance. By incorporating diverse peoples and traditions, the Persians created a model of empire that emphasized inclusivity and adaptability. This legacy of cultural assimilation and administrative efficiency can be seen in contemporary approaches to international governance and diplomacy. The ability to manage diverse populations and integrate various cultural elements remains a key challenge for modern states.

The classical empires of Greece and Rome further transformed the landscape of global power dynamics. The Greeks, with their emphasis on philosophy, science, and democracy, left an indelible mark on Western thought and political theory. The Roman Empire, known for its legal system, military strategy, and infrastructure, set the standard for centralized control and statecraft. The legacy of these empires is evident in modern political institutions, legal frameworks, and military doctrines. The principles of democracy, republicanism, and legal codification that emerged from these classical empires continue to shape contemporary governance.

The fall of these ancient empires did not erase their influence. Instead, their legacies were absorbed and adapted by subsequent powers. The Byzantine Empire, for example, carried forward the traditions of Rome while adapting to new challenges and contexts. The rise of the Islamic Caliphates, which drew upon the knowledge and innovations of previous empires, further illustrates the enduring impact of historical power struggles. These early empires provided a blueprint for future states to navigate the complexities of power, governance, and diplomacy, leaving an indelible mark on the trajectory of human history.

Chapter 2: The Rise of European Powers

The Age of Exploration and the subsequent rise of European powers marked a new era in global power dynamics. Driven by a desire for wealth, resources, and territorial expansion, European nations such as Spain, Portugal, England, and France embarked on ambitious voyages of discovery. These expeditions led to the establishment of vast colonial empires that spanned the globe, reshaping the political, economic, and cultural landscapes of the world. The legacy of European colonialism continues to influence contemporary international relations, as former colonies navigate the complexities of postcolonial identity and power dynamics.

The Iberian Peninsula was at the forefront of the Age of Exploration, with Spain and Portugal leading the charge. The Treaty of Tordesillas, signed in 1494, divided the newly discovered lands between the two powers, setting the stage for centuries of colonial rivalry and expansion. The Spanish Empire, fueled by the wealth of the Americas, became one of the most powerful entities in the world. The Portuguese, meanwhile, established a vast trading network that extended from Africa to Asia. The legacy of these early colonial empires is evident in the linguistic, cultural, and economic ties that persist between former colonies and their European counterparts.

England and France soon joined the fray, establishing their own colonial empires and competing for global dominance. The British Empire, with its vast holdings in North America, Africa, Asia, and the Pacific, became the largest empire in history. The French, with their focus on North America, the Caribbean, and Africa, also left a significant mark on the global stage. The legacy of these empires is complex and multifaceted, encompassing both the positive and negative aspects of colonial rule. The spread of Western political, economic, and cultural institutions has had a lasting impact on the development of modern states.

The legacy of European colonialism is particularly evident in the geopolitical landscape of the modern world. The arbitrary borders drawn by colonial powers have contributed to ongoing conflicts and tensions in regions such as Africa and the Middle East. The extraction of resources and exploitation of labor during the colonial period has left a legacy of economic inequality and underdevelopment. At the same time, the spread of Western education, legal systems, and administrative practices has shaped the governance and institutions of many postcolonial states. The influence of European powers is also evident in the continued dominance of Western countries in global political and economic affairs.

The decolonization process of the 20th century marked a significant shift in global power dynamics. As former colonies gained independence, they sought to assert their sovereignty and redefine their identities. The legacy of colonialism continues to shape the relationships between former colonies and their former colonizers, as well as the broader international community. Issues such as reparations, cultural preservation, and economic development remain central to contemporary debates on the legacy of colonialism. The rise of European powers and their subsequent decline has left an indelible mark on the world, influencing the trajectory of global power struggles and shaping the contours of modern international relations.

3

Chapter 3: The Ottoman Empire's Influence

The Ottoman Empire, which spanned over six centuries, was one of the most powerful and enduring empires in history. At its height, it controlled vast territories in Europe, Asia, and Africa, exerting significant influence over global trade, politics, and culture. The legacy of the Ottoman Empire continues to shape contemporary international relations, particularly in the Middle East and Southeast Europe. The administrative, legal, and cultural innovations of the Ottomans have left a lasting impact on the regions they once ruled, influencing the development of modern states and the dynamics of regional power struggles.

The rise of the Ottoman Empire began with the conquest of Constantinople in 1453, marking the end of the Byzantine Empire and the beginning of Ottoman dominance. The Ottomans established a centralized and efficient administrative system, known as the devshirme, which recruited talented individuals from diverse backgrounds to serve in the government and military. This meritocratic approach allowed the Ottomans to build a strong and cohesive state, capable of managing its vast and diverse territories. The legacy of this administrative system is evident in the modern governance structures of many countries in the Middle East and Southeast Europe.

The legal system of the Ottoman Empire, known as the Kanun, combined Islamic law with traditional and customary practices. This legal framework provided a flexible and adaptable system of governance, allowing the Ottomans to manage their diverse population effectively. The Kanun influenced the development of legal systems in many countries within the former Ottoman territories, leaving a lasting impact on their legal traditions and institutions. The emphasis on justice, fairness, and social welfare in the Ottoman legal system continues to resonate in contemporary discussions on governance and law.

The Ottoman Empire was also known for its cultural and intellectual achievements, which left a significant mark on the regions it controlled. The empire was a melting pot of cultures, languages, and religions, fostering a rich and diverse cultural heritage. The Ottomans were patrons of the arts, architecture, and literature, contributing to the development of a vibrant and cosmopolitan society. The legacy of this cultural diversity is evident in the modern cultural landscape of the Middle East and Southeast Europe, where the influences of Ottoman art, music, and architecture can still be seen and appreciated.

The decline of the Ottoman Empire in the late 19th and early 20th centuries had profound implications for global power dynamics. The disintegration of the empire and the subsequent redrawing of borders in the Middle East created a complex and often contentious geopolitical landscape. The legacy of Ottoman rule continues to influence regional politics, as countries navigate the challenges of nationbuilding, identity, and governance. The memory of the Ottoman Empire, with its emphasis on inclusivity, adaptability, and cultural richness, serves as a reminder of the complexities and possibilities of empire and its enduring impact on contemporary international relations.

4

Chapter 4: The Colonial Legacy in Africa

The colonization of Africa by European powers in the late 19th and early 20th centuries had a profound and lasting impact on the continent. The legacy of colonialism continues to shape the political, economic, and social dynamics of contemporary Africa, influencing its development and its interactions with the rest of the world. The arbitrary borders drawn by colonial powers, the exploitation of resources, and the imposition of foreign governance systems have left a complex and often contentious legacy. Understanding the colonial history of Africa is essential for comprehending the challenges and opportunities faced by the continent today.

The Berlin Conference of 18841885 marked the formalization of the "Scramble for Africa," during which European powers divided the continent among themselves without regard for existing ethnic, cultural, or political boundaries. This arbitrary division created artificial states with diverse and sometimes conflicting groups, leading to internal tensions and conflicts that persist to this day. The legacy of these colonial borders is evident in the numerous border disputes and internal conflicts that have plagued many African countries since independence. The challenge of nationbuilding and fostering a sense of national identity remains a central issue for contemporary African states.

The economic exploitation of Africa during the colonial period had far-reaching consequences for the continent's development. European powers extracted valuable resources, such as minerals, rubber, and agricultural products, with little regard for extracting maximum profits. This exploitation led to the underdevelopment of local economies and the creation of economic structures designed to serve colonial interests rather than the needs of the indigenous populations. The legacy of this economic exploitation is still evident in the economic challenges faced by many African countries today. Issues such as poverty, inequality, and dependency on primary commodities are rooted in the colonial period, and addressing these challenges requires a deep understanding of the historical context.

The imposition of foreign governance systems during the colonial period also had a profound impact on African societies. European powers introduced new administrative structures, legal systems, and education models that often disregarded or undermined traditional institutions and practices. This disruption of local governance and cultural systems created a legacy of political instability and social dislocation. The struggle to reconcile traditional governance structures with modern state institutions is a continuing challenge for many African countries. Efforts to promote good governance, rule of law, and democratic participation are often complicated by the legacies of colonial rule.

The cultural impact of colonialism in Africa is complex and multifaceted. While colonial powers often sought to impose their cultural values and practices, the resilience and adaptability of African cultures allowed for the preservation and evolution of indigenous traditions. The colonial period also led to the creation of new hybrid cultures, blending elements of African and European influences. This cultural hybridity is evident in contemporary African art, music, literature, and social practices. The legacy of colonialism in the cultural sphere is a testament to the enduring strength and creativity of African societies in the face of external domination.

The decolonization process and the subsequent struggle for independence in Africa were marked by significant challenges and achievements. The emergence of nationalist movements, the fight for selfdetermination, and the quest for political and economic sovereignty were defining features of this period. The legacy of these struggles continues to shape the identities and aspirations of contemporary African states. The experiences of colonialism and decolonization have also contributed to a strong sense of solidarity and unity among African nations, as they work together to address common challenges and assert their place in the global arena.

5

Chapter 5: The Cold War's Global Impact

The Cold War, a period of geopolitical tension between the United States and the Soviet Union, had a profound impact on global power dynamics and international relations. The ideological struggle between capitalism and communism played out on a global stage, influencing political, economic, and military developments around the world. The legacy of the Cold War continues to shape contemporary international relations, as former allies and adversaries navigate the complexities of a postCold War world.

The division of the world into rival blocs during the Cold War had farreaching consequences for international politics. The establishment of military alliances, such as NATO and the Warsaw Pact, created a polarized international system characterized by mutual suspicion and competition. The concept of containment, aimed at preventing the spread of communism, led to a series of proxy wars and interventions in various regions, including Korea, Vietnam, and Afghanistan. These conflicts left a lasting impact on the countries involved, shaping their political, social, and economic development for decades to come.

The Cold War also had a significant impact on the global economy. The competition between the United States and the Soviet Union extended to economic systems, with both superpowers seeking to promote their respective models of capitalism and socialism. The United States' Marshall Plan, for example, provided economic aid to Western European countries to help rebuild their economies and counter the influence of communism. The legacy of these economic policies is evident in the development of the global economic system, with institutions such as the International Monetary Fund and the World Bank playing a central role in shaping international economic relations.

The end of the Cold War in the late 20th century marked a significant shift in global power dynamics. The dissolution of the Soviet Union and the emergence of the United States as the sole superpower created a unipolar world order. This transition brought both opportunities and challenges, as countries adjusted to the new geopolitical landscape. The legacy of the Cold War continues to influence contemporary international relations, as former Soviet states navigate the complexities of independence and integration into the global system. Issues such as nuclear disarmament, regional conflicts, and ideological divisions remain central to international diplomacy.

The cultural impact of the Cold War is also significant. The ideological rivalry between the United States and the Soviet Union extended to the cultural sphere, with both superpowers seeking to promote their values and way of life. The legacy of this cultural competition is evident in the enduring influence of American and Soviet cultural products, from Hollywood films to Soviet literature. The cultural exchanges and interactions that took place during the Cold War contributed to the development of a global cultural landscape that continues to shape contemporary society.

The Cold War era also saw significant advancements in science and technology, driven by the competition between the superpowers. The space race, for example, led to groundbreaking achievements in space exploration, with the United States landing the first humans on the moon and the

Soviet Union launching the first artificial satellite. These technological advancements have had a lasting impact on various fields, from space exploration to communication and transportation. The legacy of the Cold War's scientific and technological achievements continues to influence contemporary research and innovation.

6

Chapter 6: The Rise of China

The rise of China as a global power in the late 20th and early 21st centuries has had a profound impact on international relations and global power dynamics. China's rapid economic growth, military modernization, and assertive foreign policy have transformed the geopolitical landscape, challenging the dominance of traditional Western powers. The legacy of China's rise is shaping the future of global politics, as countries navigate the complexities of a multipolar world.

China's economic transformation began with the implementation of marke-toriented reforms under the leadership of Deng Xiaoping in the late 1970s. These reforms, which included the decentralization of economic decision-making and the introduction of private enterprise, fueled unprecedented economic growth and development. China's rise as an economic powerhouse has had farreaching implications for global trade, investment, and economic relations. The country's integration into the global economy has created new opportunities and challenges for international economic cooperation.

The military modernization of China has also been a key component of its rise as a global power. The Chinese government has invested heavily in modernizing its armed forces, with a focus on advanced technologies, capabilities, and strategic doctrines. This military transformation has raised concerns among neighboring countries and traditional powers, leading to shifts in regional security dynamics. The legacy of China's military rise is evident in the strategic calculations and defense policies of countries in the AsiaPacific region and beyond.

China's assertive foreign policy, characterized by initiatives such as the Belt and Road Initiative (BRI), has further solidified its position as a global power. The BRI, which aims to enhance connectivity and cooperation across Eurasia, Africa, and beyond, has significant geopolitical and economic implications. Through infrastructure projects, trade agreements, and diplomatic engagements, China is expanding its influence and shaping the global order. The legacy of these initiatives is shaping the future of international relations, as countries respond to and engage with China's growing presence on the global stage.

The rise of China also has significant cultural and ideological implications. As China asserts its influence, it promotes its cultural values and governance models as alternatives to Western norms. The concept of "soft power," which emphasizes the use of cultural and ideological influence, is central to China's strategy of global engagement. The legacy of China's cultural diplomacy is evident in the growing interest in Chinese language, culture, and political philosophy around the world. This cultural influence is reshaping the global cultural landscape and contributing to the diversity of international perspectives.

The rise of China is not without challenges and contradictions. Issues such as human rights, environmental sustainability, and regional tensions present significant hurdles for China's continued ascent. The legacy of China's rise will be shaped by its ability to address these challenges and navigate the complexities of a changing global order. As China continues to rise, its impact on international relations and global power dynamics will remain a central focus of contemporary geopolitical discourse.

7

Chapter 7: The Influence of the British Empire

The British Empire, once the largest empire in history, left an indelible mark on the world, shaping contemporary international relations and global power dynamics. At its height, the British Empire controlled vast territories across Africa, Asia, the Americas, and the Pacific, exerting significant influence over global trade, politics, and culture. The legacy of the British Empire continues to resonate in the modern world, as former colonies navigate the complexities of postcolonial identity and power relations.

The British Empire's influence on global trade and economic systems is profound. The establishment of the British East India Company and the expansion of trade networks facilitated the global exchange of goods, ideas, and technologies. The British developed a system of free trade and economic liberalism that became the foundation of modern global capitalism. The legacy of this economic system is evident in the continued dominance of Western economic institutions and practices in the global economy. The principles of free trade, market competition, and economic liberalization that emerged during the British Empire continue to shape contemporary economic policies and international trade relations.

The British Empire also played a significant role in the spread of Western political and legal institutions. The introduction of Britishstyle parliamentary systems, legal codes, and administrative practices in its colonies left a lasting impact on the governance structures of many postcolonial states. The legacy of these institutions is evident in the legal and political systems of countries such as India, Canada, Australia, and Nigeria. The principles of democracy, rule of law, and constitutional governance that were introduced during the British colonial period continue to influence contemporary political discourse and practice.

The cultural legacy of the British Empire is complex and multifaceted. The spread of the English language, the establishment of educational institutions, and the promotion of British cultural values had a lasting impact on the societies under British rule. The legacy of these cultural influences is evident in the continued global dominance of the English language, the widespread adoption of British educational models, and the enduring popularity of British literature, music, and arts. At the same time, the imposition of British cultural values often led to the marginalization and erosion of indigenous cultures, creating a The complex legacy of cultural exchange and influence that continues to shape contemporary societies. Efforts to reclaim and revitalize indigenous cultures in the postcolonial era are a testament to the resilience and creativity of these societies. The British Empire's cultural legacy is a reminder of the power of culture in shaping identities and forging connections across borders.

The decolonization process and the subsequent struggle for independence were defining moments in the history of many former British colonies. The legacy of these struggles is evident in the political and social landscapes of countries such as India, Kenya, and South Africa. The fight for selfdetermination, civil rights, and social justice continues to resonate in contemporary movements for equality and human rights. The legacy of the British Empire is a complex tapestry of power, resistance, and transformation, shaping the contours of modern international relations and global power dynamics.

8

Chapter 8: The Influence of the Soviet Union

The Soviet Union, a global superpower for much of the 20th century, had a profound impact on international relations and global power dynamics. The legacy of the Soviet Union continues to shape contemporary geopolitics, particularly in Eastern Europe and Central Asia. The rise and fall of the Soviet Union left an indelible mark on the political, economic, and social landscapes of its former territories, influencing their development and interactions with the rest of the world.

The establishment of the Soviet Union in 1922 marked the beginning of a new era in global politics. The Bolshevik Revolution and the subsequent creation of a socialist state challenged the existing capitalist order and introduced a new ideological framework. The Soviet Union's emphasis on centralized planning, state control of the economy, and the promotion of socialist values had farreaching implications for international relations. The legacy of the Soviet economic model can still be seen in the economic policies and structures of many former Soviet states, as they navigate the transition to market economies.

CHAPTER 8: THE INFLUENCE OF THE SOVIET UNION

The Cold War rivalry between the Soviet Union and the United States defined much of the 20th century's global power dynamics. The ideological struggle between communism and capitalism played out in various regions, leading to proxy wars, political interventions, and the formation of military alliances. The legacy of this rivalry is evident in the ongoing geopolitical tensions between Russia and Western countries, as well as the continued influence of Cold Warera institutions and agreements. The dissolution of the Soviet Union in 1991 marked the end of the Cold War but left a complex and often contentious legacy in its wake.

The cultural and social impact of the Soviet Union is also significant. The promotion of socialist values, education, and the arts played a central role in shaping the identities and aspirations of its citizens. The legacy of Soviet cultural policies can be seen in the continued influence of Sovietera literature, art, and scientific achievements. At the same time, the repression of dissent and the imposition of state control over cultural expression left a lasting impact on the societies within the Soviet sphere of influence. The struggle for cultural and intellectual freedom remains a central issue in many former Soviet states.

The collapse of the Soviet Union led to significant political and social upheaval in its former territories. The transition to independent nationstates, the challenges of economic reform, and the quest for political stability have shaped the contemporary landscape of Eastern Europe and Central Asia. The legacy of the Soviet Union is evident in the ongoing efforts to address issues such as corruption, governance, and human rights. The memory of the Soviet era continues to influence the political discourse and identities of the countries that emerged from its dissolution.

The influence of the Soviet Union on global power dynamics and international relations is a complex and multifaceted legacy. The rise and fall of this superpower left a lasting impact on the world, shaping the contours of contemporary geopolitics and the development of former Soviet states. The lessons of the Soviet experience continue to inform debates on governance, economic policy, and international relations, providing valuable insights into the challenges and possibilities of global power struggles.

9

Chapter 9: The American Century

The 20th century is often referred to as the "American Century" due to the United States' emergence as a global superpower and its significant influence on international relations and global power dynamics. The legacy of American dominance continues to shape contemporary geopolitics, as the United States navigates the complexities of maintaining its position in a rapidly changing world. The rise of the United States as a global power has had profound implications for global politics, economics, and culture.

The United States' rise to global prominence began in the aftermath of World War II. The war left much of Europe and Asia devastated, while the United States emerged relatively unscathed and economically robust. The establishment of international institutions such as the United Nations, the International Monetary Fund, and the World Bank, with strong American influence, set the stage for a new global order. The legacy of these institutions is evident in the continued dominance of Western countries in global governance and economic systems. The principles of liberal democracy, freemarket capitalism, and international cooperation that the United States promoted continue to shape contemporary international relations.

The Cold War rivalry between the United States and the Soviet Union further solidified America's position as a global superpower. The United States' policy of containment, aimed at preventing the spread of communism, led to a series of military interventions, diplomatic efforts, and strategic alliances. The legacy of these policies is evident in the continued presence of American military bases around the world, the formation of alliances such as NATO, and the influence of American strategic doctrines. The end of the Cold War and the dissolution of the Soviet Union left the United States as the world's sole superpower, shaping the unipolar world order that emerged in the late 20th century.

The economic influence of the United States during the 20th century was unparalleled. The American economy, characterized by innovation, technological advancements, and consumer culture, became a model for development and growth. The legacy of American economic dominance is evident in the global spread of multinational corporations, the influence of the U.S. dollar as the world's primary reserve currency, and the adoption of American business practices and technologies. The principles of free trade, economic liberalization, and entrepreneurship that the United States championed continue to shape the global economic landscape.

The cultural impact of the United States during the "American Century" is also significant. The spread of American popular culture, including music, film, television, and fashion, has had a profound influence on societies around the world. The legacy of American cultural dominance is evident in the global popularity of Hollywood films, the widespread adoption of Americanstyle entertainment, and the influence of American values and lifestyles. The promotion of American culture and ideals, often referred to as "soft power," continues to play a central role in the United States' global strategy.

The legacy of the "American Century" is complex and multifaceted, encompassing both positive and negative aspects. While the United States has played a significant role in promoting democracy, human rights, and economic development, it has also been involved in controversial interventions, power struggles, and conflicts. The challenges of maintaining global leadership in a rapidly changing world, addressing issues such as inequality, climate change, and geopolitical tensions, continue to shape the United States' role in contemporary international relations. The "American Century" has left an indelible mark on the world, influencing the trajectory of global power struggles and shaping the contours of modern geopolitics.

10

Chapter 10: The Impact of Decolonization

The process of decolonization, which began in the mid 20th century, had a profound impact on global power dynamics and international relations. The struggle for independence and selfdetermination by former colonies reshaped the geopolitical landscape, leading to the emergence of new nationstates and the reconfiguration of global power structures. The legacy of decolonization continues to influence contemporary international relations, as former colonies navigate the challenges of postcolonial identity, governance, and development.

The decolonization process was marked by significant political and social upheaval. The fight for independence often involved armed struggles, mass movements, and diplomatic efforts, as former colonies sought to assert their sovereignty and break free from colonial rule. The legacy of these struggles is evident in the national narratives and identities of many postcolonial states. The experiences of resistance, liberation, and nationbuilding continue to shape the political discourse and aspirations of contemporary societies.

The emergence of new nationstates in the wake of decolonization transformed the international system. The establishment of the United Nations in 1945 provided a platform for newly independent countries to participate in global governance and advocate for their interests. The legacy of decolonization is evident in the increased diversity and representation within international organizations, as well as the emphasis on principles such as selfdetermination, sovereignty, and noninterference. The voices and perspectives of former colonies have played a crucial role in shaping the norms and practices of contemporary international relations.

The economic challenges faced by postcolonial states are a significant aspect of the legacy of decolonization. The extraction of resources and the exploitation of labor during the colonial period left many former colonies with underdeveloped economies and structural inequalities. The legacy of these economic challenges is evident in the continued struggles for economic development, poverty alleviation, and sustainable growth. Efforts to address these challenges often involve navigating the complexities of global trade, investment, and aid, as well as promoting inclusive and equitable development policies.

The social and cultural impacts of decolonization are also profound. The process of reclaiming and revitalizing indigenous cultures, languages, and traditions has been a central aspect of postcolonial identity formation. The legacy of cultural resilience and adaptation is evident in the diverse cultural landscapes of postcolonial societies. At the same time, the imposition of colonial cultural values and practices has left a lasting impact on social structures, education systems, and cultural norms. Efforts to decolonize education, promote cultural preservation, and address historical injustices are central to contemporary movements for social justice and equality.

The legacy of decolonization is a testament to the enduring power of selfdetermination and the resilience of human societies. The struggle for independence and the pursuit of justice continues to resonate in contemporary movements for equality and human rights. The legacy of decolonization is a complex and multifaceted narrative, encompassing both the triumphs and challenges of forging new national identities and navigating the global order. The experiences of decolonization have left an indelible mark on the international system, influencing the dynamics of power, governance, and development in the modern world.

11

Chapter 11: The Middle East and the Legacy of Empire

The Middle East, a region with a rich history of empires and civilizations, has been profoundly shaped by the legacy of imperial rule. The rise and fall of empires such as the Ottoman, British, and French have left an enduring impact on the political, social, and economic dynamics of the region. The legacy of these empires continues to influence contemporary international relations, as the countries of the Middle East navigate the complexities of identity, governance, and conflict.

The collapse of the Ottoman Empire after World War I led to the redrawing of borders and the establishment of new states in the Middle East. The SykesPicot Agreement, a secret deal between Britain and France, divided the former Ottoman territories into spheres of influence, creating artificial borders that disregarded existing ethnic, religious, and cultural divisions. The legacy of these arbitrary borders is evident in the ongoing conflicts and tensions in the region, as countries struggle to reconcile their diverse populations and historical grievances. The challenge of nationbuilding and fostering a sense of national identity remains a central issue for many Middle Eastern states.

The British and French mandates in the Middle East further complicated the region's political landscape. The imposition of foreign governance systems, the manipulation of local leaders, and the pursuit of imperial interests created a legacy of political instability and social dislocation. The struggle for independence and selfdetermination in the mid20th century was marked by significant challenges and achievements. The legacy of these struggles is evident in the national narratives and identities of contemporary Middle Eastern states. The experiences of resistance, liberation, and nationbuilding continue to shape the political discourse and aspirations of the region.

The economic impact of imperial rule in the Middle East is also significant. The extraction of resources, the establishment of trade networks, and the introduction of new economic models had farreaching consequences for the region's development. The legacy of these economic policies is evident in the continued dependence on oil and other natural resources, as well as the challenges of economic diversification and sustainable development. Efforts to address these challenges often involve navigating the complexities of global trade, investment, and aid, as well as promoting inclusive and equitable development policies.

The cultural and social legacy of empire in the Middle East is a complex and multifaceted narrative. The imposition of foreign cultural values and practices often led to the marginalization and erosion of indigenous traditions. At the same time, the resilience and adaptability of Middle Eastern cultures allowed for the preservation and evolution of local identities. The legacy of cultural hybridity is evident in the rich and diverse cultural landscapes of the region, where the influences of Ottoman, British, and French rule can still be seen and appreciated. Efforts to reclaim and revitalize indigenous cultures and traditions are central to contemporary movements for cultural preservation and social justice.

The legacy of empire in the Middle East is a testament to the enduring power of historical narratives and the complexities of contemporary international

CHAPTER 11: THE MIDDLE EAST AND THE LEGACY OF EMPIRE

relations. The experiences of imperial rule, resistance, and independence have left an indelible mark on the region, shaping its political, social, and economic dynamics. The challenges of navigating this legacy and forging new paths forward continue to define the Middle East's interactions with the global order.

12

Chapter 12: The Future of Global Power Struggles

The legacy of historical empires continues to influence contemporary international relations and global power dynamics. As the world navigates the complexities of a multipolar order, the lessons of the past offer valuable insights into the challenges and possibilities of the future. The rise of new powers, the resurgence of regional influences, and the ongoing struggle for dominance and cooperation shape the contours of modern geopolitics.

The rise of new global powers, such as China and India, is reshaping the international system and challenging the dominance of traditional Western powers. The legacy of historical empires provides a framework for understanding the strategies and tactics employed by these emerging powers. The experiences of imperial expansion, consolidation, and decline offer valuable lessons on the dynamics of power and the importance of adaptability, resilience, and innovation in navigating the global order. The future of global power struggles will be shaped by the ability of states to learn from the past and apply these lessons to contemporary challenges.

CHAPTER 12: THE FUTURE OF GLOBAL POWER STRUGGLES

The resurgence of regional influences and the quest for regional dominance are central aspects of contemporary international relations. The legacy of historical empires, with their emphasis on regional control and influence, continues to shape the strategies of modern states. The Middle East, Africa, and Asia are regions where the legacies of empire are particularly evident, as countries navigate the complexities of identity, governance, and regional power dynamics. The future of these regions will be shaped by the ability of states to balance the legacies of the past with the demands of the present, forging new paths of cooperation and conflict resolution.

The ongoing struggle for dominance and cooperation in the international system is a defining feature of contemporary geopolitics. The legacy of historical empires, with their emphasis on diplomacy, negotiation, and strategic alliances, provides valuable insights into the dynamics of power and the importance of building and maintaining relationships. The experiences of past empires highlight the significance of trust, mutual respect, and the pursuit of common interests in fostering stable and cooperative international relations. The future of global power struggles will be shaped by the ability of states to navigate these dynamics and build a more inclusive and equitable global order.

The challenges of globalization, technological advancements, and transnational issues such as climate change, terrorism, and cyber threats present new dimensions to the legacy of historical empires. The ability of states to address these challenges and adapt to the changing global landscape will be crucial in shaping the future of international relations. The lessons of the past, with their emphasis on resilience, innovation, and collaboration, offer valuable insights into navigating these complexities and building a more sustainable and just world.

The legacy of global power struggles is a testament to the enduring impact of historical narratives on contemporary international relations. The rise and fall of empires, the struggle for independence, and the quest for dominance and cooperation continue to shape the dynamics of global power. As the world navigates the challenges and opportunities of the 21st century, the lessons of the past offer valuable guidance for building a more peaceful, equitable, and prosperous future. The future of global power struggles will be defined by the ability of states and societies to learn from history, adapt to new realities, and forge a path towards a more inclusive and cooperative international order.

www.ingramcontent.com/pod-product-compliance
Lightning Source LLC
LaVergne TN
LVHW010442070526
838199LV00066B/6157